Dream Apartment

ALSO BY LISA OLSTEIN

POETRY

Late Empire
Little Stranger
Lost Alphabet
Radio Crackling, Radio Gone

NONFICTION

Climate (with Julie Carr)
Pain Studies

Dream Apartment

Lisa Olstein

COPPER CANYON PRESS
PORT TOWNSEND, WASHINGTON

Cover art: Nancy Mims, *Rapt Moon*, 2020. iPhone photograph on linen-cotton, antique frame, crochet yarn. 16¾ × 13¾ inches.

Copper Canyon Press is in residence at Fort Worden State Park in Port Townsend, Washington, under the auspices of Centrum. Centrum is a gathering place for artists and creative thinkers from around the world, students of all ages and backgrounds, and audiences seeking extraordinary cultural enrichment.

LIBRARY OF CONGRESS CATALOGING-IN-PUBLICATION DATA
Names: Olstein, Lisa, 1972- author.
Title: Dream apartment / Lisa Olstein.
Description: Port Townsend, Washington : Copper Canyon Press, [2023] |
    Summary: "A collection of poems by Lisa Olstein"— Provided by
    publisher.
Identifiers: LCCN 2023015201 (print) | LCCN 2023015202 (ebook) |
    ISBN 9781556596742 (paperback) | ISBN 9781619322851 (epub)
Subjects: LCGFT: Poetry.
Classification: LCC PS3615.L78 D74 2023 (print) | LCC PS3615.L78 (ebook) |
    DDC 813/.6—dc23/eng/20230410
LC record available at https://lccn.loc.gov/2023015201
LC ebook record available at https://lccn.loc.gov/2023015202

9 8 7 6 5 4 3 2 FIRST PRINTING

COPPER CANYON PRESS
Post Office Box 271
Port Townsend, Washington 98368
www.coppercanyonpress.org

Contents

\|/

/|\

\|/

/|\

\|/

/|\

\|/

/|\

Dream Apartment

FORT NIGHT

The snake is
a sleeve the deer
puts on its mouth
a beaded cuff
in the haze men
make of morning
with each release
of their fist-gripped
guns. Is this a dream
of shame is this
a dream of potential
unmet of possibility
undone? School
no pants brush
no teeth podium
no poems open
door all wall.
Dear Monster
none of the guests
we invited arrive.
In the darkness
no lion comes.

RABBIT RABBIT

I went to the city
and felt a fire
stitch into the fabric
of my days. The
crumbs I found
to eat in the crisp
gutters between
flames were good
as they burned
my throat. Tourniquet
etiquette is a way
of not bleeding
through the cloudy
bandage of each
drumming day—
no bridge of brays
and all the wrong
burrs stuck in this
coat becoming
someone else's.
The stink of a man
is a lasting kiss
when you don't
want to touch or be
touched. Evergreen
licorice is the mind

of the past

of the woods

in the wood.

ROOT

God made her
his vessel. No.
God made of her
a vessel. No.
The river poured
into her as if
a vessel. Yes.
God made of
her a raft. No.
Her child clung to
her as if a raft.
No. Clung to her
as a raft. Yes.
God made of her
a vassal. Yes
landless
river-pastured
root cut loose.

KISS

It's true I
rue. I tore
myself apart
for you and you
loved to watch
me do it loved
to watch me
crack my hips
like a whip toss
myself skyward
seeding thunder
to the clouds.
It's the brain
that feels the pain
it's the body
that delivers it.

PLUM

To the ear
plum is
indistinguishable
from *plumb*
the way love
disappears before
no one's eyes
exactly how
fathoms the line
plumbing the air
with the scent
of plums in green
morning not yet
mourning still
morning still
time.

APPARENT WINNER

Once the moon came close, brushed
its rough cheek to my face, but

before my eyes could adjust to the light
spilling gas-like, it was retreating again

into a more distant orbit. Is this where
I go when I don't want to hear

the news or what passes for its fevered
breath, did I earn this morning's calm,

no, that's the medicine I took
to stop the thoughts realistic enough

but impossible with which to sleep.
A real-life bogeyman followed me home

last night—one woman, two children—
down my own dark street, later,

something about the way with her bare hands
the chef on TV caressed the naked inside

of the slaughtered sow made watching
its body come apart into cuts all right

except for the head because the line
drawn in me is apparently the thoughts.

I don't want to take another being's life force
for my own if I don't need to is what

I said to my mother over the phone
after communing with an ant

late on a different long-ago night—
I was beautifully high

all the neighborhood cats had come out
to see me—but still I had to eat and so I ate

and since I could, I ate well. Let's
not make this about petty differences,

certain suffering limited my options.
There's so much suffering. Sometimes

I cause it, sometimes I have no choice
but to let it suckle at my breast

my pinky in a pinch, it's so hungry.
Why are you such a bad person

too often I find myself wanting
to say, also, *I love you.*

The toddler wearing a leash
designed to look like a backpack

so his mother might feel less self-conscious
has brought his horse figurines

to see the horses in their muddy pasture
on the other side of the soft-edged fence

today. I watch them through the window
of this country vet waiting room

as a burly man carries his sick dog in
and I look for them again when

he carries his dead dog out, but this time
all I count is vulture-vulture-sparrow-

hawk until the tech taps my arm
and says *you can take your cat.*

BLUE IS THE ROOM IN THE HOUSE WE DON'T USE

Thank god you're still here beats the heart
to the beloved turbulence of living air.

Wolf-spelled, I can't always tell the swallows
from the landlady's shadow until she laughs

and I think *crow-crow.* Ivory caskets
in the moonlight, creatures of what comforting

alarm before dawn, what familiar distress
in the undress of weeded lawns, here is a flock

of peonies, ants still blissful in their sticky cling
of buds. Sometimes when I make a mistake

I repeat it to be sure: *that hurts, yes,*
try again. Where I might have chosen power,

many days I chose kindness and many days
have been filled with regret. A cat will eat you

disdainfully it is said, but how is it better
for a dog to starve beside you instead—

so little of us edible, arable, in the end
but I confess, I've only ever wanted to swallow

my dead, only the closest, only to hold them
closer still. Rabbits, my doctor is my nurse.

She tells me not to watch the news anymore.
In this she echoes the advice I give myself

but I hold it against her anyway.
Rabbits, it hurts.

COME, CALAMITY

Render tender the shoots
of evening, let us in the lettuce

light, fitful as fish pumping
fistfuls of razored air, jagged

saws: tsk-tsk, cut-cut. Gleaners
in the gloaming—fuck that,

I was starving and far too far
from any lavender heroics.

There's a moment when
you realize the beloved baby's

milky paste has long since
turned to shit, another when

the smell of any man fills
the closed-off room.

Many a time called in by dark,
called in by storm, I knew

full well who it was I comforted.
Little other breathing, nothing

to do but shape myself around you
like a shell in the ordinary night.

HOST

Frozen at the sword-tipped castle gates
of *will I will I,* I grew my meager garden,

flicked worms from wasting stalks, my failing
stock stored deep in the mud's pantry.

The tide beyond the moat was beyond reach
but waves move air to ear and slowly,

slowly they reached me. The tide was people,
the people were bodies already and about to be:

masked, gowned, stripped, wrapped,
latched, gasped, towed, anchor-split

and filling like estuaries, chambers ill lit,
attic attacked, small fires spreading everywhere

and all the wrong blankets. Who feasts
this feast day? Not I, what us, how thus?

Via touch of my own hand, via droplet
laden, via particles free. Doubling time versus

half-life. Consider letting one hand
become contaminated while trying to keep

the other clean. Tick-tick, the slick whip
riding herd in the stormy terrain of the brain,

knock-knock, who's there, the wind,
the weed, the drought, the deluge, a crack

in each cell's armor, a kink in their chain.
What sorrow barge docks overnight,

what surge will dirge the shore of us,
when will its eye pass through me,

what will I see? Having not much I try
to want for less, quiet as a mouse now,

soft as a rabbit. More barren, more
barren this not-winter grows its fortress

of tawny husks. Blood thistle, bent bristle,
I grow smaller in each night's sick light,

an ember easily spun round by the whirlpool
any good fire exhales until everything

unimaginable breaks again on the sun-splashed
rock of another living day and out I go

on the occasion of a cloud, so rare
any moisture in the air, any cool hand

smoothing its blue brow. Wind, whittle me,
how I've missed your soft blades. How

many days since, how many days till, how
will we hold these losses, with both hands?

WAYS AND MEANS

A divine spark from an ocean of fire
lights up the vast night in you.

You're dragging something—
the past? This pathway is open,

that pathway is closed.
Destiny, karma, contracts,

who knows, all of your lifetimes?
Go to the space behind your eyes

that has to do with winter.
Who knows all of your lifetimes?

There. There is your despair.
Bless it with the spark.

GREAT QUESTION

When I say seeing you again really opened me up
I mean like a hatchet to the chest

I keep hidden in my chest, stuck drawers
near the heart. Little lathe, long past,

do you remember? After years of careful study
and even more studied looking away,

having retraced the memory palace
from the unfinished novel of what lives

and lives and lives and still lives
wherever it is flint meets spark in the dark,

hot orange here then gone low and slow,
a smoldering field, a controlled burn—

yes, I remember. Finally,
I've located the girl, the bend, the night,

that series of precise and fumbling distances
that set our bodies in motion

across thousands of other nights but
from these forensics I've gleaned no wisdom

only wish, sorrow, sorrow, wish,
nothing at all about the ox I am or my cart.

THE SPELL

The lover who punished me—
The sea wasp that stung me—

The mold that bloomed behind the walls that housed me—
The evil eye cast by a rival to expel me—

The love gold as any honey hived around me—
The pills I took—

The pills I didn't take—
The doctors, the needles, the vials, the scripts—

The whirring—
The silence—

The sputtering engines of my cells—

The years—
The spell I want to cast across them—

STOP IT

It's undignified, these apples
on Instagram, these owlets

in the gutter—only I could
possibly be expected to remember

what I wanted and how could I
possibly be expected to remember

so much? There's no way to tell
the wind's surface chatter

from the current's threaded pull
from the deep choreography

of bodies until the pod surfaces
one by one, staggered moons rising,

falling across the thin gray day.
Would I, yes. Can I, no.

THANK YOU GOODBYE

The way a stranded animal looks
back or circles above or reaches

a slow paw in your direction
after the terror of your carrying them

has not so much passed as is beginning to
ebb in the slipstream of their blue or green,

warm or cold blood and they can see
that what they maybe did or didn't know

to even hope for—tiniest beating wish
in the swish of the lungs—came

(as we say, not they) true or simply
that somehow by some grace they are

returned now to an element—air, water,
earth—they can recognize and though

they cannot possibly recognize you,
they recognize that you were there,

instrumental even, an instrument in this case
and the right, maybe righteous, fear

coursing through them now holds a glint
of gold like sunlight in a river of leaves—

this time a sloth, slowly, backward
from a newly gripped tree, this time

a sea turtle, cold stunned so we have to
search out the wave in its freeze-frame eyes.

TO FLEE THE KINGDOM

So spring today, bees in the bok choy
bolted yellow before we could eat it,

let them eat it instead, let them carry on
carrying its stardust from place to place,

let us all eat, come future come. Meanwhile,
the cat takes, gives a good long bath.

The birds—the birds will fill whatever gap
left them. Once we didn't name them

out of abundance, now we don't name them
out of respect for their loss, ours.

Hawks or whales? Jaguars, anacondas?
You've met yourself in the place you were afraid.

You're smart, you keep your head,
you've got the right stone. When you really look,

the enemy is not as it first appeared.
It's actually more dangerous

if the horse doesn't know what you want,
says the woman out front. I am the shining lotus

on top of the tallest mountain in the world
breathes the bay beneath her, steady on.

NIGHT SECRETARY

Which are worse to wake from
dreams of searching or dreams of finding

either way no secret door survives the light

      no stethoscoped click unlocks the safe

      no signal pulse awaits detection
      by the radio dial of my right hand
      its fine-tuning   its nervous adjustments

either way
            impossibly the sea

                therefore the air

*

Somewhere the night has hold of you

you laugh into it like a swimmer laughs
sometimes underwater or cries out

       brief burst as the body threads

              sliver breath through the silver curtain

      it rents and stitches stitches and rents

parting is to open
parting is to sort
parting is to leave

                    but to leave open or to close

*

Once I was too young too foolish
too thick in the folded fog
of what I didn't know Once

I was too weak too vulnerable
there were slings and arrows delayed
banknotes and dead dial tones faulty
wires crisscrossing unfathomable seas Once

some part of me flew out over the sea
a fragment a chunk holding some
harbor of heart or lung whatever it is
with which we beat and breathe whatever it was
turned bird wearing salt feather sleeves Once

time passed unmarked unremarked
through its net-work of wind

Once we pressed the red button each to each
each our own and our little screens froze
our little faces and we hung up the call
and alone again I peered through rain-splashed glass
as if from the inside of a crying eye or faceted gem

*

the straw-man fallacy
the bandwagon fallacy
the false dilemma fallacy
the slothful induction fallacy
the hasty generalization fallacy
the correlation/causality fallacy
the Texas sharpshooter fallacy
the anecdotal evidence fallacy
the appeal to authority fallacy
the no true Scotsman fallacy
the burden of proof fallacy
the middle ground fallacy
the personal incredulity
the you also fallacy
the fallacy fallacy

*

Night dilates

                      constricts

      night lifts its paw

                         claws out

your throat   your picket fence

               of lashes that little

                           electric shudder

      when I trip the wire

night says give it
take it
now me

how long since this hunting hound came around
how long again until he goes
ankle blades glinting in the lamplight

I want to be expert in nothing but you
not your absence many-hued
ripples ringing where the heron was before it went

*

Once upon a time for many years
through a woman a hollowness moved
like an echo bouncing off an empty aquifer's walls
like an ache deep in the root of a tooth

where was the kiss the key the potion
the portal the potsherd found by a goatherd

was there a trail leading her back
a scent drawing her forward

what is that feeling she can't put her finger on—
stepping softly across the hall to make sure the baby's still breathing
or lifting the lid in morning on the box holding the cat-shocked sparrow
nestled all night in newspaper to find whatever fate it hides—

    that feeling

      that

*

in this one we've sorted it all out our only problem is I take too long getting dressed
for dinner white blouse navy skirt something I'd never wear

in this one you write to say you're sorry about not writing of course we must sew the split
seam between us

in this one you help me right a leaning apple tree we swap a swaddled infant chest to chest
until it stumbles from its cocoon already able to walk there's a cliffside view
and three whale tails flicking from the surf down below
and other creatures maybe sharks

*

Red-tail patient in the grackled oak
sharp-shinned circling something
high above the house

do you like romantic stories
fuck you I mean me too
fuck me too

Little russet wren in the leaf pile
flag of one color chiming
in the no-wind's glittering thread

do you prefer reunions in the end
or when everyone is left bereft
beautifully burning

Restless horse in the paddock
charging the fence again
pulling up just short

of the toothed boards chest-breadth
chest-breath exhaled does it
shatter or cohere

depends on how near
train cloud from a distance
maelstrom up close

as if the right approach
will turn the gate
to gossamer

*

Look at this
                selfishness

       look at this

                    tractor beam of divine light

no more this   song of you
                            in the trees

give me a wolf
                to suckle

                    make me a wolf

*

This time through the forest says the wolf

       I will be the one to wear red

*

last night there was a bear

                                                   where

first up the mountain across the lake then cantilevering toward us you know
how fast they run swim our canoe was paddle-less we'd left them at the dock
we watched it was far away then we had a much better view then oh god my
arms whirred like mechanical oars they were very efficient but the bear was
towering the field of the lake was hers

                                    where were her young

right there

*

Hunger how could I

    like a current rearranging the waves

Hunger how may I

    like whispering into a bottomless vase

*

Sorrow what's my ration tonight

      full portion

Today

      the field to plow

The field in front to break
the plow
its blades

      what drags behind

Today

      what's it called when the sea turns to slush

*

vampire:

        holy water
        sunlight
        wooden stake through the heart

werewolf:

        wolfsbane
        silver blades
        silver bullets

siren:

        beeswax

zombie:

        destroy the brains

golem:

        transform truth into death

dragon:

        wear something shiny
        use a bow and arrow
        shoot from the sky
        rip out its heart

*

in this one you're in the forest

in this one I am

in this one woods spring up sharp and dark across the copse of my face
then comes the hatchet's song at dawn chop chop

*

Once upon a time two lovers
went their separate ways
lit by a long half light
cast from the same flame
sent out long limbed and glowing
from behind shadows bent
ahead a spark caught
like a hook in each of them
daily dragging its invisible haul

look at this
                            loyalty

          look at its
                                            lack

silent opera
                      where's your aria

what shall we
                                                        make of it

          nothing

*

Stupid steed

        longing   /   absence

     trying to reason   through

          (faulty reason   \   fallacies)

alone

    on her own

                    is

        this night secretary's work

*

ad hominem fallacy   red herring   fallacy of sunk costs
appeal to ignorance   slippery slope   bandwagon fallacy
appeal to authority   circular argument   false dilemma
appeal to pity   hasty generalization   sea-lioning
equivocation   straw-man argument   tu quoque

*

Search *The Odyssey* for night lines

[*and then at night by torchlight, she unwove it*]

[*all through the night till dawn the ship sailed on*]

[*because she dreamed so clearly in the night*]

[*if I stay up all wretched night beside this river*]

*

And transformations

       [into an ossifrage. Astonishment]

*

Work with different translations of the same line

[*There was / no need to go on those swift ships that gallop / like horses over miles of salty water.*

He had no need to go on board swift-faring ships, which serve men as horses of the deep, and cross over the wide waters of the sea.

No need in the world for him to board the ships, / those chariots of the sea that sweep men on, / driving across the ocean's endless wastes . . .

There was no need / for him to go on board swift-moving ships, / men's salt-water horses, to sail across / enormous seas.]

*

Use Sappho instead

use Sappho instead

[*all night long*] *I am aware*]

[*]*   ]

*

What does the echo decide

               describe

sadness speaks for itself

      speaks to its wound-work
      something a maggot might do quickly
      or over time the open sky

hunger

bury it and slowly it curdles
into a sweetness in the gut

      an empty pastel light
      the way a warm coat seems
      to draw around the freezing

*

Sadness   hunger   how dramatic

dawn assembles its dossier with or without us

        birdsong tracing a slow wave
         around the stadium
            lights coming up

      in this column   so many fingertips to faces

in this column   so many swinging doors

sally forth into the heartbreak of the day
what choice is there

      to extend the night

        the night won't

[*When day comes / we have to do the laundry*]

BAD ACTORS

How now this
plush struck lawn
who will trim
these hedges
who will water
this thirst? What
say you flora
of the garden of
my gut about this
glut temperature
spiking through
the scold's bridle
brace-works of
my non-mouth's
un-tongue. No more
ponytail vice grip
no more little
girl cord tripped.
Every wave spits
in the face of
its maker that is
its mother that is
the sea. Witness our
complicity a dog's
red collar its bright
blue leash tethered

now in the mind

to an invisible tree.

HORSE

I became his
horse meaning
for a minute
there I looked
promising like
a winner might
just maybe
he could drive
me someplace
special someplace
he wanted to
go or I was
already there
or if not quite
closer than
he was just then
and so valuable
or vault-able
either way hurry
up and neigh.

O MY OMEGA

I want to show you
my eye that I
for your eye that
wriggle on the line
that pitch mewing
your cry. You/me
it'll never happen
that's the arrangement
our contract of
snow-laced pine
and yellow meadow
leaking moon look
how it spends
its light all over you.
So many sirens
last night after
midnight's mad dash
and rash splash
of orange and red
and blue Omega
was that you?

PREY

I have looked

in the flashing

eyes of a man

turned animal

and fled like prey

fled his shadowed

tunnel gaze

his glinting flick

of eye and tongue

horse-like heart

pounding full

gallop faster—

my herd was small

we both ran hard

her legs were

longer we were

close enough still

for our eyes to rein

we kept running

we were lucky

horses that day

we got away.

SHOT

I'm the wet actor
on the cold stage
of November's
play of daylight
waning and they
haven't run the shot
yet and no hot
water bottles under
my gown can
stop the shivering.
My lines change
with every inch of
water crawling up
the steel skin of
this tank but plot is
useless down here
in gulps of spray
off the fake ship's
prow. Was that
tactical or was that
strategic? That was
political. The storm is
inevitable they say
the storm is coming
this way so let's
get the best shot.

EVENT HORIZON

Today's hard green fruit latched along
the length of each small branch tells me

there was a flowering I missed or moved
too quickly by to see or saw and let pass

through the net memory casts over the day
for the mind to sort through later, dreaming.

Loquat, what? Mulberry, ok.
Tomorrow's nine months since you stopped

your ticking clock. What I most can't stand
to see is your body coming at me

in pictures: sunny porches, golden necks
arched a little in laughter, saying nothing

about what we did and didn't know.
This morning, astronomers confirmed

with a telescope called Event Horizon
something about relativity, capturing

the first-ever images of an actual black hole
fifty-three million light-years away

and one-and-a-half light-days across.
Light days: is there anything more beautiful?

Event horizon: a region in space-time
beyond which events cannot affect an outside observer

or the point of no return or the boundary at which
gravity's pull becomes so great there's no escape.

HELLO, BROTHER

Did you walk out the front door of yourself,
stunned magnolia in the hailstorm,

nurse nerves first fled down a tunnel
of false fountains marking the route?

Too often, the snapshots parading across
my dreams are stock characters of a forgettable

day but last night finally you came through,
dead but whole, cheerfully turning knobs,

looking for the door you were meant to enter—
fern and conch mathematics, vestibular,

auroral. This morning, once again, all America
has one son the chorus sings because

finding he could not run, a boy threw himself
through a tunnel of air to tackle the nightmare

(nightly, a mare) in whose line of sight he found
the breath of his life standing, but sons are not

interchangeable and no love is like any other:
the what of you, the here, the sway.

THE DISASTER AGAIN

The intensity of it, that distantness
that keeps watch. Bereft of light,

absence refers endlessly to the other
law, the disaster again in motionless

flight: the four winds from nowhere,
the night, the lure of it, the night,

the thought of it, disastrous already.
Dreaming, something wakes, a sliding

half gleam in a devastated field,
disastrous return. Then we who are

turned away from the star wake gently.
That there is nothing disastrous in this

is surely what we must learn to think.
This, too, is fatal or, as they say, inevitable—

the absence linked to the disaster, fragmentary,
posterior to every possibility yet to come.

AND THEN FOREVER

You became a question

    exploding on our tongues

        tearing at the soft flesh of any

            pink chamber left—your name

                a shattered mirror a rogue wave

            a cocked gun. Rabbits are back

        reads the butcher's sign not

    for signaling spring is fleet-

footed but for meat to eat.

MATERIAL FACTORS

We grow tired of news

    from the interior when

        news from the interior

            is the only news we know.

                From the interior: same fixed

                    lotto it always was—some cells

                        dance in error some cells bounce

                  as usual unless until who knows?

                The interior is slow to reveal itself

            except when it's a gushing rush

        or feather dry and barely a

    rustle just a quick twig snap

of an iridescent throat.

KINDER SEA

There in the trembling port

    of morning who knew yet what

        wriggled in the net pulled in the

            predawn and slapped down on

                the rough dock of fuel-flowered

                    air? What motor failed in you

                        overnight what failure did you

                            read in us before after turning out

                      the light—was there a raised lip

                you stepped over a plank you

            crossed a gap you leapt did you

        even notice it did you turn around

      to toss a coiled rope did it feel

    like a moment of pulling into

or pushing off from shore?

YOUR NAME HERE

At first the dog can't believe her luck

    but soon wearies at the weight of what

        she finds herself trying to pull us through

            and before long even peering across this

                milky scrim—what is it sadness suspended

                    so cold it burns—is exhausting. When

                        we go how long do we exist in her mind

                            is she out of practice now that we never leave

                      or is she more practiced than ever coming

                  to the ghost-gate of us the almost-us but pale

              and wavering that greets her everywhere like

            the same name uttered sometimes is a sail

        sometimes a solemn nation a nationless flag

      a shiftless shield a battering ram a lack of

movement in the trees not like that like this

ALL THIS BRITTLE LACEWORK

Outstretched in the too many

    too thin arms of the battled tree

        an explosion of fragments—each

            hooked husk the twisted fist of a hard

                brown thought a barbed question the

                    nuthatch meant to leave unanswered

                        —what difference can this knowing

                    make what meager meal of it are we

                supposed to take under all this brittle

            lacework sprung fractured fractally

        razor-reasoned in the forensic film

    we pore over all winter pretending

space in a crowded cloud.

ONLY A FLAWED HUMAN IS YOUR JUDGE

Forgive me for turning

    away from this particular

        heartbreak today there is

            no repair wafting in on the

                air nothing but dragons

              firebreathing deep in their—

        stop rhyming—as if to sing-

    song my way out—of

what—my deepest rut.

HAPPY NEW YEAR

Is it selfish to wish for more than to survive?
I see you, bare arms gleaming in the sun-

struck snow, I see the browned roast
you brought to your wine-stained lips,

the stack of books you read, and those boots
that last fall you loved yourself in.

I see you in them again on this roll call
morning stroll through what intimate data

strangers tell me about their lives.
Once upon a time I asked them to

or they asked me, who can recall,
I'm into it, I guess. I like to watch,

at least, I can't seem to stop, but I can't
bear to share, so I'll tell you here:

the cat finally came home last night—
spooked by so many fireworks barking,

he hid somewhere unsearchable for a while
no matter how I called and called.

He chose me, I like to say since the day
I found him starving on the porch.

I know the night is full of unsteady boats
on cold seas and horrible cages

and people far more alone than me.
I'm sorry for your loss, your cancer,

the accident you had no way to see coming
and the one you did have an inkling of,

I've learned how important it is to say
because of how difficult it is to say

and how loudly loneliness fills the silence
although, like anything, it depends—

for instance, I still can't unhitch my breath
from even the softest whisper of your name.

OUR CITY HAS BECOME A SERIES OF ISLANDS

My mother believes the dead
need the grieving, without them

hover conscripted, a congregation
of ghosts. Do you see them, how

does it make you feel, I don't allow
myself to ask. Help me, please

help me, is the beggar's refrain
on the F train today. Do you

hear him, we agree across the rows
with our eyes not to ask, how

does it make you feel? With no one
to mourn for them, she says, to wash

and wrap their bodies and pray
over them before placing them

in the freshly dug dirt, they are
straight-stuck dolphins stranded

by some hunger or tide. Aboveground
tracks have a way of reminding us

how many waterways bracelet
the island's narrow wrist, the city

already its own map of thresholds
crossed. How does it make you feel?

AS FOR REAL WOLVES

A bear's body freezes after being shot
by a hunter a friend says a friend

learned from a video and only recoils
after the threat is gone. You try

using your sociological imagination
when you're face down frozen by fear

in the performance of your life for your life
(places, everyone) or by some other measure

of the ambient air. I get the funniest feeling
sometimes—a kind of visual grammar

the cast of light in actual photons, something
moving with force, just in case or

just in time. *Take your art into the narrowest places*
the dead man said *and set yourself free.*

GLACIER HAIBUN

In one chemical future, the clouds themselves will be extinct, so we try
to hold them in mind as they float by casting their individual storm-sized
shadows across the animals across the plains. *Ground,* the ranchers call
it: grazing heads on, moving herd over, pieces of. Outside the park, fast-
growing calves summer-nurse in the same coulees they tumbled onto,
tundra then, thirty below and nine months before the feedlot of November.
Inside the park, brown bears lumber up and down mountains they were
herded into to make room for this steered prairie, for men and merchants
and meat, and every lodgepole pine they twist their bodies around set forth
from a seed spun out at a hundred and thirty degrees—every inch of this
ground once ablaze, then, their straight lines tell us.

The lake last night was the best painting I've ever seen.

Maybe he wanted to disappear, N. says to the ranger in line for coffee just back from a three-day shift on Search and Rescue. That's not what his people say, she answered. But they'd probably be the last to know, N. muses back at the cabin, not noticing the shiver it sends through us, the slack parachute misfiring again above our heads—the one we want to cut the cord from but can't. All the songs on your playlist are built around a pedal point, D. tells me (petal point, I mishear), a few days later as we drive under it through a carefully labeled Forest in a mostly mapped Wilderness to visit B. in his chemical present (chemo). An unmoving bass note anchors the shifting chords, he says, it's a way to build tension and release.

Animal, adjust, says the voice in my head.

The same racist neighbors who refer to the Obama presidency with a vile slur are the ones who hauled water to them, unasked, when their well went dry, who plowed the no-plow road twice a day during his six-week radiation commute, who didn't tell him his medical bills were what the green beer and corned beef fundraiser were for until they dropped off the cash, B. tells us over dinner, dismayed, embarrassed. It's a friendly place to live, if you're white. Across the valley, the canola field's electric yellow drains the just-bloomed sweet clover of all its light. Closer in, the Monsanto new product tester's square green fields leak chemicals into the wind. He's a true believer, thinks he's going to feed the starving world, B. reports. What happens next, I ask hours later gesturing weakly toward the crises, the crossroads, the whatever-you-want-to-call-it we've been circling for hours. What happens next, he repeats, what happens next is what we do.

Animal, adjust.

Like a wave of pleasure rippling down a cat's back under the touch of his favorite hand. Like a river meeting a shelf of rocks strangely pitched, a tumble of stones, not knowing which way to flow, so circling for a moment, a concentration, a furrowed brow of pool, before finding gravity again, its irrefutable logic. Like seeing the hands of a woman you love reaching skyward through a stand of lilacs she planted as a break against the wind. Like a killdeer dragging its wing across the dusty road, *over here, over here,* to herald herself a better meal than her eggs over there, *don't look over there.* Like a child who hasn't won anything in this game of trading presents, who for one golden moment held something he wanted, something he thought for a flicker might be his to keep, but the game went on, he had to pass it to the next set of sticky hands, he had to watch it land in someone else's grasp.

Magpie, killdeer, curlew, meadowlark, marsh hawk, common merganser, bald eagle, golden eagle, osprey, crow, raven, swallow, seagull, sandhill crane. (This isn't a bucket list, it's a thank-you note.)

Inside the park, the mountain goats licking something mineral off the road cutbanked and precipitous aren't tame so much as practical. Summer is short, all ode and elegy: the sweep of burned mountain across the lapis lake is spiked with distant spears, Bluebeard bristles—the lodgepole trunks all that remain and first to return, ghost-masts of ships long gone or just arriving. The man is still missing; Search and Rescue gives way to Search and Recovery. Outside the park, the news is still bad; heat waves, bullets, overturned tankers. You want to ignore it, maybe for a little while think in geologic time or the flow and freeze of a river, a glacier, but the rocks are touched, the river is touched, the glaciers are sooty and melting. You're never actually away, you're just adjusting your altimeter again. "How to travel without getting lost," the manual instructs, is the mission: "travel journal, slice of life, everything seen through the author's eyes." Set a mood, it suggests, interrupt it often, write in both past and present tense, end with a surprise—the essence is cutting.

Meanwhile I lift my glass to these black-and-silver striped nights. I believe that the rain never drowned sweeter, more prosaic things than those we have here, now, and I believe this is going to have to be enough.

ANIMAL

Ok so you're
a lynx your
babies are hungry
but it's cold outside
your den do you
stay inside where
it's warm or do you
go out looking
for food ok so
you find some food
left over from wolves
but it's heavy
do you go on
searching or do you
try to drag it back
to your den ok
so while you're
dragging it back
to your den you
encounter a bear
do you stay and
fight or do you
call for help ok
no one hears you
do you stay and
fight or do you

run back to your

den ok good

choice you make it

back to your den

but your babies

are starving.

SEE IT

A heart attack is
private. A riptide is
public sometimes
look at the chain
beachgoers make
of their arms.
A drive-by is well
from what cracked
window do you peer?
See it: witness
survive it: victim
succumb to it:
deceased dear released
do it: perp.
We all have lists
to make knife
to skin begins one
a surgeon sitting
next to me both of us
rehearsing fix-it jobs
five miles high
in the crowded sky.
Fix it: I can't
fix it: we won't.
I've always wanted to
die here I meant

as measure as ode

when I said it

lovingly to the sea

now streaming

concrete beneath me.

Ok says the sea

meaning literally.

MOTHER NORTH

How are you
feeling are you
outside what
is that the birds
are so loud

says my mother

the North watching

chickadees silent

in late winter snow

to her daughter

the South where

sun-soaked doves

coo and trill from

the fence separating

neighbor East from

neighbor West both

of us wearing masks

of distance greedy

and discrete as

the crow in his tree

sounds like the cardinal

my son waking

calling out *Mom*

Mom from the swirling

center of a wind rose

or the unmapped

side of a moat but
isn't. *Mom I didn't*
call for a symptom check
me to her bouncing
between silver not-
stars. *Mom what's*
your temperature
him to me sailing
his small craft into
the mercury light.

SPRING

Scene summary
a dog a Dalloway
units larger than
a pinprick smaller
than a hedgerow.
If gold is the product
of two stars colliding
what is it we wrap
around our ribboned
necks? At night
we lay down our
glinting heads: here.
Hear hear exhorts
the chorus *there there*
soothes the soft voice
of the house in the
house of memory.
A chapter is an epoch
and an economy
of scale. A spring is
a coil a small stream
a source sprung
by a season (here)
and leapt (there).

GROUP PORTRAIT 1244403

The archival body
has a complicated
history with numbers.
Numbers themselves
are a kind of archive.
History is a kind of
body. Bodiless memory
archives architected time.
Early on maybe a robin
later perhaps a rabbit.
Out of order she fell
in love with a boy some
twenty years too early
or late. *I'll howl like a wolf*
you howl like a coyote
the boy said *so we can*
find each other in the woods.
Despite all appearances
to the contrary the archive
has few rules: presence
stands in for absence
darkness stands in
for light shape stands in
for body a silhouette is
the shadow's revenge.

NOTES

"Ways and Means" and "To Flee the Kingdom" are indebted to Rivers Sterling. "Animal" is indebted to Toby Goodrich.

"Night Secretary" quotes several lines from Homer's *The Odyssey,* translated by Emily Wilson. Alternate translations of a single line were pulled from several public domain sources found online. The poem also quotes a fragment of Sappho, translated by Anne Carson in *If Not, Winter.*

"Event Horizon" and the other poems in the book's fifth section are for Ian Kennedy, in loving memory.

"Hello, Brother" takes its title from the greeting given by a worshipper at the Al Noor Mosque in Christchurch, New Zealand, to the stranger who then opened fire, killing forty-four people.

"The Disaster Again" collages phrases from Maurice Blanchot's *The Writing of the Disaster,* translated by Ann Smock.

The italicized line in "As for Real Wolves" is borrowed from Paul Celan's "The Meridian."

The italicized line in "Glacier Haibun" is borrowed from John Ashbery's "Haibun 6." The poem, also indebted to Margaret Chula's "Guidelines for Writing Haibun in English," is for Billy Conway, in loving memory.

ACKNOWLEDGMENTS

Thank you to the editors and staff of the publications that first featured some of these poems (sometimes in earlier versions): The Academy of American Poets Poem-a-Day, *American Jewish History, The Baffler, Bennington Review, The Best American Poetry* blog, *Colorado Review, Foundry, Inner Forest Service, ISLE: Interdisciplinary Studies in Literature and Environment, jubilat, The Massachusetts Review, Narrative,* and *A Public Space.*

Thank you to the John Simon Guggenheim Memorial Foundation, Rude Mechs, and the University of Texas at Austin's research fellowship program for the invaluable support of time and space. Thank you to the Office of the Vice President for Research, Scholarship and Creative Endeavors of the University of Texas at Austin for their subvention grant in support of this book's production.

Thank you to Michael Wiegers, essential editor and friend, and to everyone at Copper Canyon Press for incomparable care and feeding over the years and in this instance. Thank you to Nancy Mims for permission to use *Rapt Moon* on the cover of this book and for her exquisite work.

Thank you to Jane Miller and Julie Carr for being cherished and indispensable first and final readers for this work while in progress. To Elizabeth McCracken, Deborah Paredez, Kris Delmhorst, Noy Holland, and Cecily Parks for vital encouragement and insight along the way. To each of the above and to Heather Abel, Edward Carey, Rob Casper, Jennifer Chang, Liz Cullingford, Lauren Dias, Jeffrey Foucault, Carrie Fountain, Heather Houser, Peter Kochansky, Lisa Moore, Domino Perez, Adam Zucker, and Leni Zumas (×2) for sustaining friendship, collaboration, inspiration, and/ or support in work, art, life, or any combination of the three. Thank you to David and Toby, to my parents, Linda and Michael Olstein, and to the rest of my family for everything.

ABOUT THE AUTHOR

Lisa Olstein is the author of five poetry collections published by Copper Canyon Press: *Dream Apartment, Late Empire, Little Stranger, Lost Alphabet,* and *Radio Crackling, Radio Gone.* Her nonfiction includes *Pain Studies* (Bellevue Literary Press), a book-length lyric essay, and *Climate* (Essay Press), an exchange of epistolary essays co-written with Julie Carr. Olstein is the recipient of a Pushcart Prize, Lannan Residency Fellowship, Writers League of Texas Discovery Prize, Hayden Carruth Award for New and Emerging Poets, and fellowships from the John Simon Guggenheim Memorial Foundation, the Sustainable Arts Foundation, and the Massachusetts Cultural Council. Currently, she is the Ellen Clayton Garwood Centennial Professor of Creative Writing at the University of Texas at Austin, where she teaches in the New Writers Project and Michener Center for Writers MFA programs.

Poetry is vital to language and living. Since 1972, Copper Canyon Press has published extraordinary poetry from around the world to engage the imaginations and intellects of readers, writers, booksellers, librarians, teachers, students, and donors.

WE ARE GRATEFUL FOR THE MAJOR SUPPORT PROVIDED BY:

academy of american poets

THE PAUL G. ALLEN FAMILY FOUNDATION

amazon literary partnership

POETRY FOUNDATION

4 CULTURE

Lannan

the point
envision·enact·evolve

ART WORKS. National Endowment for the Arts arts.gov

WASHINGTON STATE ARTS COMMISSION

A&
OFFICE OF ARTS & CULTURE
SEATTLE

The Witter Bynner Foundation for Poetry

TO LEARN MORE ABOUT UNDERWRITING
COPPER CANYON PRESS TITLES,
PLEASE CALL 360-385-4925 EXT. 103

WE ARE GRATEFUL FOR THE MAJOR SUPPORT PROVIDED BY:

Richard Andrews and
  Colleen Chartier
Anonymous
Jill Baker and Jeffrey Bishop
Anne and Geoffrey Barker
Donna Bellew
Will Blythe
John Branch
Diana Broze
John R. Cahill
Sarah Cavanaugh
Keith Cowan and Linda Walsh
Stephanie Ellis-Smith and
  Douglas Smith
Mimi Gardner Gates
Gull Industries Inc.
  on behalf of William True
William R. Hearst III
Carolyn and Robert Hedin
David and Jane Hibbard
Bruce S. Kahn
Phil Kovacevich and Eric Wechsler

Lakeside Industries Inc.
  on behalf of Jeanne Marie Lee
Maureen Lee and Mark Busto
Ellie Mathews and Carl Youngmann
  as The North Press
Larry Mawby and Lois Bahle
Hank and Liesel Meijer
Petunia Charitable Fund and
  adviser Elizabeth Hebert
Madelyn S. Pitts
Suzanne Rapp and Mark Hamilton
Adam and Lynn Rauch
Emily and Dan Raymond
Joseph C. Roberts
Cynthia Sears
Kim and Jeff Seely
D.D. Wigley
Barbara and Charles Wright
In honor of C.D. Wright,
  from Forrest Gander
Caleb Young as C. Young Creative
The dedicated interns and faithful
  volunteers of Copper Canyon Press

The pressmark for Copper Canyon Press
suggests entrance, connection, and interaction
while holding at its center
an attentive, dynamic space for poetry.

This book is set in Arno Pro.
Book design by Phil Kovacevich.
Printed on archival-quality paper.